SIMBA DREAMS OF KIBBLES
Published by SAADO CAVALIER and ALEJANDRA CAVALIER

Copyright ©2021 SAAD JALLAD. All rights reserved.

No part of this book may be reproduced in any form or by any mechanical means, including information storage and retrieval systems without permission in writing from the publisher/author, except by a reviewer who may quote passages in a review.

All images, logos, quotes, and trademarks included in this book are subject to use according to trademark and copyright laws of the United States of America.

JALLAD, SAAD, Author
SIMBA DREAMS OF KIBBLES
SAAD JALLAD

ISBN: 978-0-578-84145-8

JUVENILE FICTION / Animals / Baby Animals

All rights reserved by SAAD JALLAD, SAADO CAVALIER and ALEJANDRA CAVALIER.
This book is printed in the United States of America.

SIMBA

BELLA

ALEJANDRA

SAADO

Once upon a time...

There was a little King Charles Cavalier puppy named Simba.

Simba loved to play, dream, and go on wild adventures.

Simba lived at the Winston House Apartments in Foggy Bottom with his mother, Alejandra, his father Saado, and his best friend, Bella.

These are their stories...

Chapter 1

Simba Dreams of Kibbles

It was a beautiful Sunday morning in Foggy Bottom, and the Cavalier family were waking up at their Winston House apartment.

"Get ready or we are going to be late for our reservation!" announced Saado.

"Good morning! Where are we going for Sunday brunch today?" asked Alejandra.

"Why Fogo de Ciao, of course, my love," replied Saado.

"FOGO DE CIAO!" yelled Simba, "That's the Brazilian restaurant with the never-ending kibbles! I'll go get ready."

While Simba was getting ready, Saado and Alejandra walked out the door. "I'm ready!" shouted Simba, "Hey, where did everybody go?"

"They already left," said Bella as she lunged into a downward dog stretch on her yoga mat.

"Bella, you aren't coming. There won't be enough kibbles for you," snapped Simba as he scratched at the door.

"I thought you said the kibbles were never-ending," wept Bella. "Oh, pretty please, can I come, Simba?"

Simba paid little attention to her as he continued to scratch at the door.

"They probably went to order ahead," concluded Simba, "I'll just wait here until they come back for me."

"Don't fall asleep like last time," giggled Bella.

"Nonsense!" replied Simba, "Sleeping is for puppies, and I'm a big dog. I'll lay here for a minute until they..."

Simba fell into a deep sleep, and Bella curled up next to him.

"Sweet dreams, big dog," chuckled Bella.

"Ahem, señor..." said a voice with a thick Spanish accent. "Ahem, señor Simba," the voice repeated.

Simba opened his eyes to see a small man with a moustache, dressed in black with a white apron and chef's hat.

"Good morning, Cavalier family, and welcome to Fogo di Ciao. Yo soy Lazaro and I am your server today. Is your first time?"

"No, Lazaro, we were here last weekend," replied Alejandra, "Don't you remember?"

"Oh sí, sí, sí," confirmed Lazaro. "How could I forget, señora?"

"We love this place," said Alejandra. "The food is so good, and the ambiance is beautiful."

"Not as beautiful as you, my darling," alleged Saado.

"Ok!" said Lazaro after an awkward pause, "Then you know how it works. This green circle 🟢 means kibbles come, and this red circle 🔴 means kibbles no coming."

"I'll just have a green circle, please," decided Simba.

"Que?" said Lazaro, looking worried.

"Only the green circle for me, Lazaro. Thank you," repeated Simba.

"A Dios mio! Not again!" moaned Lazaro, as he granted Simba's request. It delighted Simba. One by one, the waiters came by and served an assortment of kibbles: pink ones, blue ones, and Simba's favorite red ones.

Simba ate and ate and ate. He ate so much that he blew up like a balloon. He got bigger and bigger until he was as big as a small house!

"Simba, that's enough!" scolded Alejandra. "You won't fit through the door again!"

"But Mom, we didn't even get to dessert yet," pleaded Simba.

"Surely he can have a little dessert Alejandra," laughed Saado. "It won't make a difference now, anyway,"

"Hush, Saado," interrupted Alejandra. "Lazaro, could you give us a hand?"

"Sí, sí, sí, señora, but of course," obliged Lazaro.

Lazaro, Alejandra, and Saado rolled Simba out of the restaurant until Simba got stuck in the doorway.

"Simba!" called Bella with concern. "Simba! You're stuck in the doorway. Are you ok?"

"Quite comfortable, actually. I think I'll take a nap," mumbled Simba as he drifted off into a deep sleep.

"Simba!" said Bella, "Simba, wake up! You're dreaming again!" yelped Bella while tugging at his ear.

Simba woke up from his dream when the door opened.

"Hey guys!" said Alejandra, as she kneeled down for hugs and kisses.

"Guess what we brought for you from Fogo Di Ciao?" announced Saado, holding a bag up in the air.

"KIBBLES!" shouted an overjoyed Simba and Bella.

Chapter 2

The Case of the Missing Kibbles

"Bella!" yelled Simba.

"Bella, come to the kitchen. Quickly!" commanded Simba.

"Coming!" said Bella in a muffled voice with crumbs all over her face and something hiding behind her back.

"Bella, something terrible has happened," declared Simba, worried.

"Gulp," swallowed Bella. "Umm... what happened?" inquired Bella nervously.

"Someone has stolen yesterday's left-over kibbles," claimed Simba, pointing to an open and empty pantry.

"Oh, my word," squealed Bella as she wiped crumbs from her face. "Whatever shall we do?"

"Not to worry, Bella," comforted Simba. "This is a job for detective Simba."

"Detective Simba to the rescue!" said Bella proudly, as she nuzzled Simba.

"I say... what do you have there hidden behind your back?" asked Simba suspiciously.

"Oh, nothing at all," Bella lied as the front door opened.

"Eiiiiiiiiii hey Simba & Bella. It's me, Dean, da handyman of da Winston House."

"It was Dean!" barked Bella, pointing at Dean. "Dean stole the kibbles!"

"Well, well, well, Mr. Dean," Simba said suspiciously. You do have a spare key to our apartment, don't you? How do we know that you didn't take our beloved kibbles?"

"Eiiiiiiiii it wasn't me little Simba. You see, my wife prepares ma lonch for me every day of da week," explained Dean.

"And what exactly did she prepare today?" asked a hungry and curious Simba.

"Eiiiiiiiii she prepared fufu and goat liver stew," replied Dean.

"Bella, go get ready," urged Simba. "We have to find those missing kibbles, or else it's goat liver stew for lunch."

"Eiiiiiiiii well, good luck to you, little Simba. Betta ask Addison if someone turned in da kibbles at da reception."

Down the elevator went the pups. The elevator door opened in the lobby, and there was Addison attending the reception.

"Good morning, Simba & Bella," waved Addison. "How are you today, pups?" he asked, while processing an Amazon parcel.

"It was Addison!" barked Bella, pointing at Addison. "Addison stole the kibbles."

"Well, well, well, Mr. Addison," Simba said suspiciously. "What are in all those Amazon boxes, I wonder?" Perhaps our beloved kibbles are in there?

"Oh, no, Simba," replied Addison. "That's not possible. "Amazon doesn't mail out perishable items like kibbles. But if you need some, then head down to Trader Joe's market down the street. They will have some there."

The two pups thanked Addison and scampered out of the Winston House on to Trader Joe's.

"Jump in the shopping cart, Bella, and I'll push it," instructed Simba. "When we get to the kibbles section, fill her up!"

"Aye aye, captain," saluted Bella as she jumped up into the shopping cart.

"There they are," pointed Bella. "Right after the frozen section."

Bella quickly tossed several boxes of kibbles into the cart until it was full.

"Ready to check out Simba," confirmed Bella.

Simba pushed the cart to the front of the checkout line and recognized the cashier immediately.

"Hey Lazaro," waved Simba. "Working at Trader Joe's today?"

"It was Lazaro!" barked Bella pointing at Lazaro. "Lazaro stole the kibbles."

"No, no, no, Señorita Bea," said Lazaro. "Too many kibbles here. No need take yours," explained Lazaro with a chuckle. "Son 100 dollars, Señor Simba."

"What?" gasped Simba. "But I don't have any money."

"Lociento Señor Simba. But if you no have no money, I no can give you kibbles," explained Lazaro.

"What treachery is this?" roared Simba. "Kibbles should be free of charge for all pups!"

"Yeah!" agreed Bella. "That way you could steal as many kibbles as you want, Lazaro!"

"Sí, sí, sí," agreed Lazaro. "Free kibbles es bueno. You can go tell the judges at the Supreme Court. They make the rules. Take these with you."

Lazaro pulled two white curled wigs from the mannequin heads, gave them to Simba and Bella, and wished them well.

"I still think it was Lazaro," proposed Bella as she walked out of Trader Joe's with the missing kibbles still hiding behind her back.

Chapter 3

The Supreme Court

The Cavalier family were having breakfast. It was a big day for Simba. He was going to the Supreme Court to ask the judges to pass a law that would make kibbles free for all pups.

"Good morning, pups!" said Alejandra as she sipped her coffee. "Where did you get those silly wigs?" asked Alejandra, laughing uncontrollably.

"Lazaro gave them to us at Trader Joe's," answered Simba.

"Oh, that's odd," said Alejandra. "Why would he do that? They look like the wigs that the Supreme Court judges wear. Enjoy your breakfast!" she said as she walked out the door.

"Have a good work-day, my darling," said Saado to an already shut door. "What's on the agenda today, pups?"

"Simba is going to plead his case to the Supreme Court today," boasted Bella.

"Oh, that's great, Simba!" encouraged Saado. "Go make history, guys."

Down the elevator went the pups. The elevator door opened in the lobby. There was the building manager, Michael, dressed in a tight designer black suit with a rainbow-colored handkerchief.

"Addison, there is a car in the garage that is not registered in the system," hissed Michael in a condescending and nasal voice.

"Did you want me to locate the owner, Michael?" asked Addison.

"No, I want you to boot his car," snapped Michael. "And fine him 100 dolla, ok?"

18

"Hey, pups," waived Addison. "Cool wigs you got there!"

Michael turned around, saw the pups, and nearly gagged.

"There are no dogs allowed in the Winston House," yelled Michael. "Addison, fine them 100 dolla!"

"We are service dogs," said Simba.

"And what service do you provide?" asked Michael.

"We provide hugs and kisses," replied Bella, looking pleased with herself.

"Charming," said Michael sarcastically. "Identification?"

Simba and Bella pulled their identification cards from their harnesses and handed them to Michael.

"Bella, if he doesn't allow us to pass, you know what to do," whispered Simba.

"I sure do," yelled Bella.

"You can't be out and about without your parents, you stupid dogs," scolded Michael as he returned their identifications. "Return home immediately before I have you for lunch!"

"Now, Bella! DOWNWARD DOG!" shouted Simba.

Bella scampered behind Michael and lunged into the downward dog yoga position. Simba jumped up at Michael like an eagle, ready to pounce. Michael cried out like a little girl and tripped over Bella. The pups ran over Michael and out the door.

"Addison," called Michael from the floor. "When those pups get back here, fine them both 100 dolla!"

"Sure thing, Michael," replied Addison, trying to keep a straight face.

The pups were on their way.

"That was great!" praised Bella, galloping alongside Simba.

"There it is," shouted Simba, pointing towards the Supreme Court.

20

"There is a police officer at the entrance," said Bella. "How are we going to get in?"

"Darn," said Simba. "I thought they abolished the police in Foggy Bottom."

Simba surveyed the area and saw a familiar face.

"Look, there's Lazaro," said Simba. "Maybe he knows a way in."

Lazaro was rolling a garbage cart towards the pups with purpose. He already seemed to know the problem and wanted to help.

"Señior Simba," called Lazaro. "I work today Supreme Court. Quick jump in basura. You too, Señorita Bea."

"You want us to jump into the garbage bins, Lazaro?" asked a confused Simba.

"Sí, sí, sí señior," replied Lazaro. "Policia no see you. You go Supreme Court. Ask free kibbles."

The pups jumped into the garbage bins and rolled in past the officer into the building undetected.

"Wow! Thanks, Lazaro," said Simba. "Where do we go from here?"

"Los tea personas, Los tea personas," replied Lazaro as he pointed to two men dressed in black robes and grey wigs down the hall.

"What in the world are 'Los tea personas'?" asked Simba.

"Judge Edmund, how do you do?" said Alastor in a deep ghostly voice. "Did you have your tea today?"

"Oh, Judge Alastor, good day. Yes, I most certainly did have my tea," confirmed Edmund.

"Splendid Judge Edmund," cheered Alastor. "One lump of sugar or two, old boy?"

"Quick Bella, those judges must be 'Los tea personas'," claimed Simba. "Let's follow them into the Supreme Courtroom."

The two judges continued to talk about tea as they walked into a full courtroom and started the hearing.

"We are gathered here today for a very important matter," Edmund addressed the audience.

"Tea," interrupted Alastor stupidly.

"Quite right," confirmed Edmund. "We must open our borders, to cheap labor, from horrible lands, to farm our tea plantations, so we can acquire all the riches..."

"Bella, now is our chance," whispered Simba. "I'll distract them while you circle around, then downward dog them like you did Michael."

"I'm on it," yelled Bella.

Bella scampered under the judge's legs and waited for Simba's signal.

"Judge Edmund!" screamed Simba. "Would you care for some tea?"

Edmund looked down from the podium.

"Who the devil are you?" asked Edmund.

"I'm Simba from the Simba Tea Company. I'm here to sell you everlasting tea bags."

"Everlasting tea bags, you say?" asked a curious Alastor. "Maybe we should give the pup a listen, Edmund. I have never heard of an everlasting tea bag before."

"That's because everlasting tea bags do not exist, you buffoon!" jeered Edmund. "Guards! Remove this vile beast from my sight!"

"DOWNWARD DOG Bella, now!" yelled Simba.

Bella lunged into position as Simba pounced on the judges sending them down onto the floor.

"Oh bugga," said the fallen judges.

"The stage is yours, Simba," said Bella. "Go get em, big dog!" she smiled.

24

"I had a dream," preached Simba to a shocked crowd, "that one day, all kibbles, would be free kibbles for all pups. Oh yes, I had a dream today! We pups give you free hugs. We pups give you free kisses. Now you people give us free kibbles!"

The crowd erupted and threw their wigs into the air! They cheered so loud the room shook.

"Order! Order!" grumbled Edmund as he got up from the floor. "The people have spoken. From this day forth, till our last, kibbles will remain free of charge for all pups."

Simba and Bella jumped in the air and embraced each other with joy.

"Can we take off these wigs now?" asked Bella.

Chapter 4

A Christmas Kibble

'Twas the night before Christmas, and Alejandra was reading a bedtime story to the pups.

"And so, as Tiny Tim observed, God bless us, everyone," read Alejandra.

"Mom, Simba slept through the story again," said Bella with a chuckle.

"Oh, he was awake for parts of it," replied Alejandra. "Leave him be, Bella."

"Bah, Humbug," Simba muttered in his sleep as he dreamed.

The doorbell rang at the Simba Tea Company. Saado looked through the window to see who was at the door.

"It's Christmas carolers, Mr. Simba," said Saado with delight. "Shall I let them in, sir?"

"Tell those singing beggars to leave at once," said Simba. "Then return immediately to work for which I pay you handsomely."

"Yes, sir, right away, Mr. Simba," said Saado.

Saado opened the door, and the carolers burst into the room and sang before he could stop them.

"Christmas is coming," sang the carolers. "The goose is getting fat. Please to put a penny in an old man's hat. If you have no penny, then kibbles will do. If you have no kibbles, then God bless you."

"Stop, stop, stop," yelled Simba. "No, gooses! No, pennies! No, kibbles!" You singing beggars get out at once," screamed Simba as he pushed them out and slammed the door.

28

"Come now, Mr. Simba," said Saado. "They are cold and hungry, and it's Christmas."

"Poor excuse for picking my pocket every 25th of December," said Simba. "Old Judge Edmund and Judge Alastor would have sent them off to jail if they still ran this company."

"But 'tis the season of giving, sir," said Saado as he put another coal on the fire.

"Come over here, Mr. Saado," commanded Simba.

Saado walked over to a stern-faced Simba sitting in an old chair that was much too big for him.

"What is this?" asked Simba, holding his shirt.

"A shirt," answered Saado.

"And this?" asked Simba, holding his coat.

"A coat," answered Saado.

"And this?" asked Simba, holding his top hat.

"A hat," answered Saado.

"These are clothes, Mr. Saado," explained Simba. "Once purchased, they can be used indefinitely. Coal burns. Coal is momentary, and coal is costly. There will be no more coal burned in this office today. Is that quite clear, Mr. Saado?"

"Crystal clear," said Saado as he put on his coat.

"I will be off then," said Simba. "And don't lock up a moment earlier, Mr. Saado."

"Don't you worry, sir. I'll stay till closing," assured Saado.

Simba walked out the door to a snow-ridden pavement. At the Simba Tea Company corner was a frail little pup with wheels attached to her hips to help her walk.

"Merry Christmas, Mr. Simba," said little Bella."

"Don't beg on this corner, girl," said Simba.

"I'm not begging, sir. I'm little Bella. I'm waiting for my father, Saado."

"Hmm," said Simba. "Saado is your father, ay? Well, then you will have a long wait, won't you?"

"Thank you, sir," said little Bella.

"Humbug," said Simba as he walked off.

As afternoon turned to dusk, Saado finally locked up the Simba Tea Company and saw Little Bella waiting patiently at the corner.

"And what do have we here," said Saado gazing at his little girl.

Bella blushed and started pacing in circles with uncontrollable excitement.

"Did Santa send his most beautiful reindeer to escort me home this Christmas evening?" asked Saado.

"No, Daddy. It's me, little Bella," giggled Bella.

"Oh, it's you, isn't it?" said Saado. "Could I get a ride, anyway?"

"You're too big, Daddy," replied Bella laughing.

"Well, in that case, hop on for the ride, beautiful," instructed Saado as he scooped up little Bella and put her on his shoulders.

"Let's get home before old Mr. Simba puts me back to work," said Saado as they walked back to their very humble home.

Chapter 5

The Judges' Warning

Simba was walking through a bustling market in the town on his way home. Everyone was out shopping for last-minute Christmas presents. In the distance a familiar face was approaching.

"Hey, Mr. Simba!" called Addison from across the cobbled road.

"Oh no," Simba said to himself. "That buffoon is going to ask me for money again."

Simba ignored Addison's call and tried to avoid him unsuccessfully.

"Great to see you, Mr. Simba," said Addison as he shook Simba's paw.

"The feeling is not mutual," replied Simba. "Now, kindly allow me to pass."

"At this festive season of the year," said Addison, "it seems desirable that those of us with means should make some slight provision for the poor and destitute who suffer greatly at this time."

"Are you seeking money from me, Mr. Addison?" asked Simba.

"Many thousands need common necessary and common comforts," said Addison.

"Are there no poorhouses?" asked Simba. "No charity centers or prisons you can put them all in?"

"They are all very full, sir," replied Addison. "A few of us are raising money to buy the poor some food, drink and warmth. How much can I put you down for, sir?"

"Nothing," replied Simba. "I have already made kibbles free for all pups, and my taxes help support the public institutions which I have mentioned. Those who are badly off must go there."

34

"Many can't go there, and many would rather die," said Addison.

"If they would rather die, then perhaps they had better do so and decrease the surplus population," suggested Simba.

"Surely, you don't mean that Mr. Simba," said Addison.

"With all my heart," said Simba. "Now I will let you go about your business, Addison; allow me to go about mine. Good day."

As Simba neared home, it became darker. A cool gust of wind knocked Simba's hat to the floor.

"I suppose the wind wants a donation as well?" Simba said to himself.

"Simbaaaaa," howled a ghostly voice.

"Who's there?" said Simba as he turned around.

"Simbaaaaa," howled the voice again.

"What do you want?" questioned Simba. "If you would like to make a tea purchase, then I suggest you contact Saado in the morning. Thank you."

Simba arrived at his doorstep and unlocked the door when he saw two faces appear on the door knocker. They were the faces of his deceased business partners, Judge Edmund and Judge Alastor.

"Edmund?" said Simba. "Alastor? Is that you?"

Simba quickly opened the door. To his disbelief, he saw the two ghosts of his former business partners hovering over him.

"Ooooooooow Simba," howled Alastor as he waved his stubby hands in the air, trying to appear frightening. "Ooooooooow," he howled again.

"We aren't meant to scare him, you buffoon," said Edmund.

"But ghosts are meant to be scary, old boy," said Alastor, enjoying every moment.

"Why have you come back to haunt me, judges?" asked Simba.

"We have come to warn you of your imminent doom," replied Edmund.

"Go on, Spirit," said Simba. "You have my attention now."

"Half your life, you supported the poor and those who cared about you most," spoke Edmund. "The other half was consumed by riches and greed."

"Your fate will be determined by three ghosts that will visit you tonight," interrupted Alastor, still waving his hands stupidly in the air. "Either you will become the pup you once were, or you will spend your lifeless days as we do - alone to walk the earth and enslaved to useless riches until the end of time."

"The choice is yours," stated Edmund as he faded away.

"Beware, Simba," warned Alastor as he grabbed a cup of tea from the table. "Bewaaaaaaare," he repeated and faded away.

Chapter 6

Alejandra's Christmas Present

"Humbug," muttered Simba. "Absolute nonsense. All that tea has driven them mad, even in the afterlife."

Simba put on his pajamas and hopped into bed. The judges' words troubled him, although he would never admit it.

As the clock struck twelve, a gust of wind circled the room, and a bright blue light shined from the window as a figure formed.

"Are you the ghost whose coming was foretold to me?" asked Simba.

"Eiiiiiiiii, I am," replied Dean. "I am da Ghost of Christmas Past."

"Whose past?" asked Simba.

"Eiiiiiiiii your past little Simba, I have come to save you from yourself. Grab my arm, and away we go," replied Dean.

Simba did as the ghost said, and the two hovered to a different time.

"Hey, I know this place," said Simba. "I grew up here. This is the Winston House Apartments!"

"Eiiiiiiiii it is," confirmed Dean. "Christmas Day 12 years ago, to be exact."

"Look, there's mom waiting by the door," pointed Simba. "My goodness, how young she was. Come Ghost, let's go surprise her. Hey Mom!" yelled Simba to a very young-looking Alejandra.

Simba jumped into Alejandra's arms but glided right through her.

"Eiiiiiiiii she can't see, hear, or feel you, little Simba," explained Dean.

"Why not?" asked Simba

40

"Eiiiiiiiiii because we are ghosts," replied Dean. "We are only seen when we wanna be."

"Alright. Well, what are we doing here, then?" asked Simba.

"Patience, little Simba," said Dean. "Patience."

The doorbell rang. Alejandra opened the door. Addison was there holding a large package.

"Your package arrived, young lady. I have a feeling you are going to like what's inside. Merry Christmas, Alejandra." wished Addison as he set the package on to the floor.

Alejandra opened the front latch of the package. Out walked a frightened and tiny King Charles Cavalier Spaniel. Alejandra picked him up and held him close to her heart.

"Merry Christmas, Simba," whispered Alejandra.

Baby Simba instantly fell in love with his new mom and licked her face.

"I remember that day," said Simba with regret.

"You two were inseparable," reminded Dean. "There was a lot of happiness in dat home in da years to come."

"I haven't seen her in ages, Ghost," said Simba sadly. "What happened to her?"

"Eiiiiiiiiii, after you left to start da Simba Tea Company she locked herself in her room and neva came out. She didn't want to live a life without you, Simba."

"But...but... I sent her money and kibbles every year!" Simba stuttered.

"Money can't buy everything, little Simba," said Dean. "It can howeva make you very comfortable while being miserable. Your departure destroyed her."

"Stop! Stop! Stop!" yelled Simba, enraged. "No more, Ghost! I can't bear it. Leave me be!"

The two faded away, and Simba found himself back in his bed.

42

Chapter 7

Feliz Navidad

The clock struck one.

"Awful Ghost," said Simba. "How dare he show me such horrible things? The next one surely won't be so bad."

A gust of wind again circled the room, and a bright green light shined from the window as a figure formed.

"Right on time," complimented Simba. "Saado could learn a thing or two from these ghosts.

"Are you the Ghost of Christmas Present then?" asked Simba.

"Sí, sí, sí,señor," replied Lazaro.

"And where are we going, Ghost?" asked Simba. "Fogo de Ciao?"

"No, no, no, señor," replied Lazaro. "Fogo de Ciao closed Christmas. We go to Casa de Señor Saado."

Lazaro took Simba's paw, and the two hovered off to a different time.

"This isn't Saado's house, Lazaro," said Simba. "We are outside of the Simba Tea Company. This must be earlier today. Look, there's that beggar girl, Little Bella, waiting for her father at the corner," pointed Simba.

"Sí, sí, sí, Señor Lociento," apologized Lazaro. "My mistake, I take a wrong turn. Take my arm, and we go Casa de Saado."

"Wait," said Simba. "I want to see myself come out the door."

Sure enough, Simba saw himself walk out of the Simba Tea Company. "Merry Christmas, Mr. Simba," said little Bella."

"Don't beg on this corner, girl," said Simba from earlier today.

"Gosh, I'm handsome," bragged Simba. "Lazaro, tell Simba from earlier today to take another route home to avoid that pesky Addison."

"No es possible, Señor Simba," said Lazaro. "They no hear us."

"What is that beggar girl doing here, anyway?" asked Simba. "Doesn't she have to be at work or school?"

"No, no, no, señior," said Lazaro. "Nobody go school Christmas, and nobody work Christmas. Only Señior Saado work Christmas. No bueno Señor Simba."

"Oh, that's right. I made him work on Christmas. Perhaps I should have given him the day off," acknowledged Simba with guilt.

"Sí, sí, sí, Señior," agreed Lazaro. He then grabbed Simba's paw, "Vamonos!"

Lazaro and Simba flew over the town like a rocket, en route to Saado's home as a bright red light appeared on the horizon.

"What's that? Looks like a red star," yelled Simba, trying to be louder than the headwind.

"No, no, no," said Lazaro. "És Papá Noel."

"Papá, no what?" asked Simba.

The shining object was no star. It was a red sleigh pulled by eight reindeer. The driver was a massive man with a great white beard, rosy cheeks, and a deep, powerful voice.

"Hello, Lazaro," bellowed the driver.

"Humbug," whispered Simba slowly in disbelief.

"Hola Señior Papá Noel," waived Lazaro.

"Is that Simba you got there with you?" asked Santa.

"Si, si, si, señior," said Lazaro. "És Simba."

"Hello, Simba," said Santa. "I have been following your story, boy."

Simba couldn't muster the words to reply. Instead, he stared at the Christmas Spirit with his mouth open.

Santa reached into his pocket and took out a glowing rose gold coin. He flipped the coin, and it made its way to Simba's paw.

Simba gazed at the magical coin.

"You can use this coin to make one wish," said Santa. "I will grant this wish as long as the wish benefits someone else."

"Couldn't I wish a small something for myself as well?" inquired Simba.

"It doesn't work that way, boy," replied Santa, amused. "Remember, Simba, the greatest gift in the world is giving."

"Is that why you're so happy all the time, Santa?" asked Simba.

"Ho, Ho, Ho," laughed the spirit. "Indeed, my little friend."

The sleigh veered away.

"Oh, and don't let the last ghost scare you, boy," added Santa. "His bark is worse than his bite. "Good luck, little friend."

The sleigh faded off into the distance as Lazaro and Simba arrived at Saado's house. They glided into the living room where Saado and Bella were having Christmas dinner.

"Let's eat, Father," suggested Bella. "I'm starving!"

"Yes, darling," said Saado. "After we say grace and thank those responsible for this Christmas feast."

"Ok, Daddy," smiled Bella.

Saado proudly opened the platter placed in the middle of the table. On the platter was a tiny and overcooked goose. It was hardly big enough to feed a mouse.

"Now hold your water glass high in the air so I can propose a toast to the person responsible for our shelter and Christmas dinner," said Saado. "To Mr. Simba Cavalier."

Saado drank his water, but Bella refused.

"Why aren't you drinking, girl?" asked Saado.

"Forgive me, Father," apologized Bella. "But I hate Mr. Simba. Our goose is tiny. We are drinking water instead of wine. There is no coal to revive the fire. He has all the money in the world and pays you almost nothing! And worst of all, he made you work on Christmas!"

"I'm sure he has his reasons," murmured Saado.

"The goose is a bit small, isn't it, Ghost?" said Simba.

"Si, señor," agreed Lazaro.

"I'll send for a larger goose - the largest one. In fact, I'll send for barrels of wine and mountains of coal to Saado's house, Lazzaro," said Simba.

"Si, si, si, señor!" said an overjoyed Lazaro.

Simba pulled out the Santa coin and held it high in the air.

"And that beggar girl, I mean little Bella - I WISH SHE WILL WALK ON ALL FOUR LEGS AGAIN," yelled Simba as lightning struck and thunder roared.

"Gracias a Dios!" shouted Lazaro. "Los tea persona's plan is working!" he joyfully screamed into the raining sky.

"Not yet, Lazaro," hissed a condescending and nasal voice.

50

Chapter 8

The Last Ghost

Suddenly the room turned dark, and Saado and Bella disappeared. A gust of wind circled the room, and a figure dressed in a black robe emerged from the depths

"Run, Simba," commanded Lazaro. "Run now! I protect you!"

"How noble of you, Lazaro," said the spirit. "Noble and foolish."

The spirit extended his arm and pointed his crooked fingers at Lazaro. A black beam shot out of the spirits' long fingernails and sent Lazaro flying through the roof far off into the black sky.

"You know who I am, boy?" asked the spirit.

"Yes, Spirit," said Simba, trying to appear brave. "You are the Ghost of Christmas Yet to Come. Shall I take your arm?"

"Ha, Ha, Ha, Ha!" cackled the Evil Spirit. "We aren't going anywhere, boy. This will all be over very soon. Behold the next Christmas in this cursed home!" screeched the ghost as he quickly waved his sickle.

The room lightened. It was the next Christmas. Saado appeared weak and devastated. He was sitting in the same chair as he had been a year ago. Little Bella, however, was not at her chair. Instead of the little pup sat the wheels that once allowed her to move around.

"Where is Little Bella?" Simba asked with concern. "She must be walking again. That's why her wheels are not with her. Isn't that so, Ghost?"

"Ha, Ha, Ha, Ha!" cackled the spirit. "Walking? Little Bella is no more, boy. And Saado will lock himself in this very room today and I will come for him soon."

52

"NO, SPIRIT!" yelled Simba. "IT CAN'T BE ! I WON'T ALLOW IT!"

"What do you care, boy?" taunted the ghost. "If they are to die, then let them die and decrease the surplus population."

"Nooooo!" yelled Simba.

Simba attacked the ghost with everything he had, but it was useless. The spirit slowly pointed his crooked fingers at Simba. A black beam shot out of the spirit's long fingernails and suspended Simba in midair.

"Now, it's time for you to join those tea-loving friends of yours," hissed the ghost. "What a shame, boy, you almost made it. Have a nice trip."

The spirit raised his sickle, ready to send Simba to his doom.

Simba shut his eyes tight, fearful for his life. When he closed his eyes, he saw Saado hovering over him with Dean and Lazaro at his side.

"Be brave, Simba," said Saado. "Help is on the way. Open your eyes, my boy."

Simba, comforted by his father's words, opened his eyes and saw a beam of red light approaching the window like a fireball. The ball got bigger and bigger and wasn't slowing down.

"NOOOOO!" shrieked the ghost. "Not you!"

Santa and his powerful reindeer stormed through the roof and ran over the ghost.

"You didn't play fair, Michael," thundered the powerful Christmas Spirit. "Simba became the pup he had once been and he deserved another chance at life."

"Need a lift, Simba?" asked Santa.

"YES!" yelled Simba, overjoyed.

Simba jumped first onto the leading reindeer's snout and then was catapulted onto Santa's lap.

54

"Next stop, Foggy Bottom!" bellowed the Christmas Spirit. "Rudolf, Schrodinger, fly!"

"Santa!" called the trampled ghost. "When you get back, I'm gonna fine you 100 dolla."

The sleigh took off as quickly as it landed, and the two were off.

Chapter 9

I'm always with you

"That was great, Santa!" praised Simba. Where are we going now?"

"Now that you have become the pup you once were, it's only fitting that you go back to the home you once had," said Santa.

"The Winston House," said Simba.

"Quite right, boy," confirmed Santa. "There it is just up ahead."

"Santa, can I ask you a question?" said Simba.

"Sure," replied Santa, "but you only get one, boy."

"Is this all a dream?" asked Simba.

"Ho, Ho, Ho!" laughed the spirit. "Yes, you are dreaming, but this is all real, boy. You are in another dimension," explained the spirit. "An alternate reality of things that could have been."

"Why did you save me?" asked Simba.

"Ho, Ho, Ho!" laughed the spirit again. "That's two questions, boy. Ask your Father. I suspect he might know."

"Now I have a question for you," said Santa.

"Go on," said Simba, flattered.

"Do you know how to fly, boy?" asked Santa.

"No, I haven't learned yet," replied Simba.

"Well, now is your chance," bellowed Santa as he tossed Simba off the sleigh towards the Winston House.

"I am going to miss you, Simba," said the laughing Christmas Spirit.

Simba glided through the air, into the Winston House, and back into his body.

"Open your eyes, boy," said Saado.

Simba looked up and saw his family gathered around him.

"Bella," yelled Simba with glee. "You're alive! All your legs are working fine!"

"Of course I am silly," said Bella as she playfully kicked Simba with her hind legs. "Why wouldn't my legs be working?" she asked as she nuzzled him. "And why weren't you waking up?"

"Mom," yelled Simba as he jumped into Alejandra's arms. "You unlocked yourself out of your room!" rejoiced Simba as he showered Alejandra with kisses.

"Ha, Ha, Simba, what's gotten into you, boy?" asked Alejandra. "What's this all about? We were trying to wake you for hours, but you wouldn't wake up." Were you having a bad dream?"

"No, Mom," said Simba. "I was in another dimension in time. An alternative reality where I was very, very rich. Nobody liked me because I was greedy, and I hated Christmas and poor people. My deceased business partners warned me that three ghosts would visit me in the night, and they would decide my fate. Either I would be damned to roam the Earth forever with my useless riches or I would turn into the pup I once was and live to give another day. The first two ghosts were friendly, but the third one tried to kill me. Next, Santa ran over him with his sleigh, gave me a ride home, and threw me back into my body."

There was a slight silence in the room, but then Bella and Alejandra burst into uncontrollable laughter. They laughed so hard, their tummies hurt.

"Ha, Ha, Ha," laughed Bella. "You're so funny, Simba. Hey, Mom, why don't you go lock yourself in your room forever, and I'll roll off with my wheels into another dimension," joked Bella.

The girls continued to laugh. Simba sadly walked over to Saado, who wasn't laughing. "You believe me, Dad. Don't you?"

"Of course I do, son," replied Saado, giving Simba confidence and comfort.

"You do?" asked Simba, surprised. How come, Dad?"

Saado reached into his pocket. He took out a glowing rose gold Santa coin identical to the one Santa had given Simba. Saado flipped the coin, and it made its way to Simba's paw.

"You got one, too?" marveled Simba.

"Yes, son," smiled Saado.

"But...but how?" stuttered Simba.

"You have some ghost friends that are quite fond of you," explained Saado.

"Dean and Lazaro," confirmed Simba. "They brought you the coin and warned you. You wished for the Christmas Spirit to save me, didn't you?"

"Clever boy," smiled Saado.

"And you were there with me when the Evil Spirit was ready to send me to my imminent doom?"

"Yes, son," smiled Saado.

"I knew that was you and not a dream," stressed Simba. "How did you manage that, Dad? How did you manage to be there with me?"

Saado picked up his little son and gazed into his beautiful brown eyes.

"Simba," said Saado, "Wherever you are, I'm always with you, my darling boy."

The End

In loving memory of my darling boy
10% of proceeds will be donated to the Mighty Hearts Project
on Simbas birthday every 10th of December
www.mightyheartsproject.org

Made in the USA
Middletown, DE
26 November 2021